STERILISE THE DENTURES, I'M

OVER

60

WIT AND WISDOM FOR
THE YOUNG AT HEART

STERILISE THE DENTURES, I'M

OVER

60

WIT AND WISDOM FOR
THE YOUNG AT HEART

First published in the United Kingdom
by Baker & Taylor in 2014

Packaged by Susanna Geoghegan

Arrangement ©2014 Susanna Geoghegan

Manuscript by 'Roffy'

Illustrations by Jon Davis

Design by Milestone Design

Layout by Bag of Badgers

Printed in China

DISCLAIMER

The following quotes and one-liners
on turning 60 have been assembled
from the sharpest minds in the
world especially for you.

They may suggest that all 60-year-
olds are slowing down, falling apart
and at war with the world.

However, we know that you are
an exceptional person and none
of them apply to you...

You know you are 60 when you see your favourite childhood toy on Antiques Roadshow.

The writing on the wall means the grandchildren found the crayons.

One of the delights of being a senior citizen is that it's easy to annoy young people.

Step one: get in the car.

Step two: turn the indicator on.

Step three: leave it on for 50 miles.

DAVID LETTERMAN

Why do they give you a watch **when you retire** when it's the first time in your life you **don't care** what time it is?

You know you are 60 when your mind NOT ONLY WANDERS, sometimes it LEAVES COMPLETELY.

One time a guy handed me a picture of himself, and he said, "Here's a picture of me when I was younger" ...

EVERY PICTURE OF YOU IS OF WHEN YOU WERE YOUNGER.

MITCH HEDBERG

There are some who start their retirement long before they stop working.

ROBERT HALF

I felt a TREMENDOUS SADNESS for men who can't deal with a woman of their own age.

MICHAEL CAINE

My grandmother was a
VERY TOUGH WOMAN.
She buried three husbands and
TWO OF THEM were just napping.

RITA RUDNER

They call me "EXPERIENCED". Isn't a raisin just a grape with experience?

Old age: I fall asleep during THE FUNERALS of my friends.

MASON COOLEY

A couple in their 60s started to text each other on their phones. The wife decided to send her husband something romantic:

If you are sleeping. send me your dreams.

If you are laughing. send me your smile.

If you are eating. send me a bite.

If you are drinking. send me a sip.

If you are crying. send me your tears.

The husband wrote back:

I'm on the toilet. Please advise.

I'm losing my PUNCH and gaining a PAUNCH...

LIFE IS A MODERATELY GOOD PLAY WITH A BADLY WRITTEN THIRD ACT.

TRUMAN CAPOTE

Because of Mozart, it's all over after the age of seven.

WENDY WASSERSTEIN

We are born naked, wet and hungry. Then things get worse!

The first half of life consists of the capacity to enjoy without the chance; the last half consists of the chance without the capacity.

MARK TWAIN

I WAS BORN IN THE YEAR OF OUR LORD ONLY KNOWS.

Three things happen when you get to my age. First your memory starts to go – and I've forgotten the other two.

DENIS HEALEY

I USED TO THINK I'D LIKE LESS GREY HAIR. NOW I'D LIKE MORE OF IT.

RICHIE BENAUD

Age is the first limitation on roles that I've ever had to encounter. and I hit that a while ago.

JACK NICHOLSON

I try to treat each evening and weekend as little slices of retirement because no one is guaranteed a lengthy one at the end of their career.

MIKE HAMMAR

Even modern science cannot rescue one from old age.

Adults are just obsolete children and THE HELL WITH THEM.

DR. SEUSS

Age doesn't really matter; what matters is how long you've been that age.

You are
not 60,
just 50.00,
PLUS VAT.

When tyre
makers turn
60, they
lose their grip.

I'm 59 and people
call me
MIDDLE-AGED.
How many
118-YEAR-OLD MEN
do you know?

BARRY CRYER

WHY DID THE ASTRONAUT RETIRE? HE WAS SPACED OUT.

Dying while young is a boon in old age.

JEWISH PROVERB

You know you are 60 when the most IMPORTANT THING to look for when shopping IS A BENCH.

It is easy to become a monk in one's old age.

ETHIOPIAN PROVERB

You know you are 60 when you refer to anything as the **"OLDEN DAYS".**

At 60 years old your birthday suit needs REGULAR IRONING.

Life begins at forty – that means you're ONLY 20!

You know you are 60 when your HEELS GET LOWER and your SKIRTS GET LONGER.

You're never too old to learn something stupid.

I've told so many lies about my age I don't know how old I am myself.

RUBY WAX

WHEN CALENDAR DESIGNERS TURN 60, THEIR DAYS ARE NUMBERED.

Two old golfers:

"My eyes aren't what they used
to be. Did you see where
my ball went?"

"YES, BUT I FORGOT ALREADY."

You know you are 60 when
the SAGA catalogue starts
to LOOK INTERESTING.

As I get older, the years just FLY BY. I don't think there was an APRIL THIS YEAR.

JEREMY HARDY

I once wanted to save the world.
Now I just want to leave the room
WITH SOME DIGNITY.

LOTUS WEINSTOCK

NEVER PASS A BATHROOM.

PRINCE PHILLIP

When our vices desert us, we flatter ourselves that we are deserting our vices.

FRANÇOIS DE LA ROCHEFOUCAULD

You know you are 60 when you sign up to FACEBOOK to help your kids REMEMBER YOUR BIRTHDAY.

I complain that the years fly past, but then I look in a mirror and see that **very few of them actually got past.**

ROBERT BRAULT

The reason grandparents and grandchildren get along so well is that they have a **COMMON ENEMY.**

SAM LEVENSON

Old people really do have a secret though. You wanna know what it is? LUCK.

CRAIG FERGUSON

OLD WINE AND FRIENDS IMPROVE WITH AGE.
ITALIAN PROVERB

You know you are 60 when you spot the first grey hairs on your children.

WHEN ACCOUNTANTS TURN 60,

THEY DEPRECIATE.

You know you are 60 when you go to evening classes to learn and not to go for a drink afterwards.

After a man passes sixty, his mischief is mainly in his head.

WASHINGTON IRVING

Youth is the time of getting, middle age of improving, and old age of spending.

ANNE BRADSTREET

I was getting dressed and
a peeping tom looked in the
window. took a look and
PULLED DOWN THE SHADE.

JOAN RIVERS

When you're a young man, Macbeth
is a character part.
When you're older, it's a straight part.
LAURENCE OLIVIER

I RANG THE ENEMA HELPLINE. THEY SOON TOLD ME WHERE TO STICK IT.

If a man is bald in front, he's a thinker.
If he's bald in the back, he is a lover.
If he's bald in front and back,
he thinks he's a lover.

I enjoy waking up and not having to go to work. So I do it three or four times a day.

GENE PERRET

You know you are 60 when you stop calling it a tracksuit and start calling it a lounge suit.

"Papa, are you growing taller all the time?"

"No my child. Why do you ask?"

"The top of your head is poking up through your hair."

I've still got it. but nobody wants to see it.

I'M SIXTY YEARS OF AGE. THAT'S 16 CELSIUS.

GEORGE CARLIN

A man at sixty realises that his grandfather was not so old when he died at 80.

One of the greatest pleasures of growing old is looking back at the people you DIDN'T MARRY.

ELIZABETH TAYLOR

It's hard to say when one generation ends and the next begins, but it's somewhere around NINE OR TEN AT NIGHT.

CHARLES RUFFING

You know you are 60 when you're GROUNDED FOR SEVERAL DAYS after flying for just one night.

You know you are 60 when your birthday cake is

50% WAX.

The mind that is wise mourns less for what age takes away; than what it leaves behind.

WILLIAM WORDSWORTH

YOU KNOW YOU ARE 60 WHEN
YOU WRITE A NOTE
TO YOURSELF REMINDING YOU
NOT TO TAKE A SLEEPING PILL
AND A LAXATIVE
ON THE SAME NIGHT.

Then there was the woman who was cured of her nervousness in one treatment. The doctor told her it was A SIGN OF OLD AGE.

I'M NOT BALD, I HAVE flesh-coloured hair.

My hot flush just set off the SMOKE ALARM.

Life is like a maze in which you try to avoid the exit.

I guess I don't so much mind being old, as I mind being

FAT AND OLD.

BENJAMIN FRANKLIN

You know you are 60 when you look down at your watch three consecutive times and still don't know what time it is.

IT'S EASIER TO PUT ON SLIPPERS THAN TO CARPET THE WHOLE WORLD.

AL FRANKEN

When bridge players turn 60, they need a good hand.

Who is a piece of stick in youth will be a block of wood in old age.

ESTONIAN PROVERB

I've watched so many episodes of Bargain Hunt and Countdown, I think I'm due an honorary degree in MEDIA STUDIES.

My wild oats have turned into

SHREDDED WHEAT.

It's every woman's tragedy, that, after a certain age, she looks like a female impersonator. Mind you, we've known some lovely female impersonators, in our time.

ANGELA CARTER

He who devotes SIXTEEN hours a day to hard study may become at SIXTY as wise as he thought himself at TWENTY.

MARY WILSON LITTLE

I HAD AMNESIA ONCE – OR MAYBE TWICE.

YOU'RE NOT 60, JUST 6 PERFECT 10s!

When tailors turn 60, they become

MOTHBALLED.

Children are a great comfort in your old age – and they help you reach it faster. too.

LIONEL KAUFFMAN

You know you are 60 when you have a party and you don't wake the neighbours. Or your dog.

YOU KNOW YOU ARE 60 WHEN A "25 YEARS AGO TODAY..." COLUMN IN THE NEWSPAPER SEEMS 15 YEARS TOO SOON.

With my sunglasses on,
I'm Jack Nicholson.
Without them,
I'M FAT AND 60.

JACK NICHOLSON

When cricketers
turn 60,
they go
BATTY.

Give me chastity
and continence,
but not yet.

SAINT AURELIUS AUGUSTINE

Three comforts of old age:
FIRE, TEA AND TOBACCO.

WELSH PROVERB

At 60, two of the most important things in life are BOWEL MOVEMENTS and nose hair.

GREG TAMBLYN

We virtually never feel our age, but thinking that we should can lead to disaster.

MARTHA BECK

I'm pushing 60. That's enough exercise for me.

MARK TWAIN

Youth is a disease from which we all recover.

DOROTHY FULHEIM

THE BEST WAY to get most husbands to do something is to suggest that perhaps they're TOO OLD TO DO IT.

ANNE BANCROFT

I'VE HEARD THAT MEN ARE LIKE FINE WINE.

They begin as grapes, and it's up to women to stomp the hell out of them until they turn into something acceptable to have dinner with.

JILL SHALVIS

It's sad to grow old, but nice to ripen.

BRIGITTE BARDOT

I was born old and get younger every day. At present I am SIXTY YEARS YOUNG.

HERBERT BEERBOHM TREE

I have reached an age when I look just as good standing on my head as I do right side up.

FRANK SULLIVAN

Life is like a hot bath. It feels good while you're in it, but the longer you stay in, the more wrinkled you get.

When
WEATHER FORECASTERS
turn 60,
THEIR RAIN IS OVER.

I REFUSE TO ADMIT I'M MORE THAN FIFTY-TWO, even if that does make my sons ILLEGITIMATE.

NANCY ASTOR

THE ERROR OF YOUTH is to believe that intelligence is a substitute for experience, while THE ERROR OF AGE is to believe experience is a substitute for intelligence.

LYMAN BRYSON

My husband's idea of

A GOOD NIGHT OUT
is
A GOOD NIGHT IN.

MAUREEN LIPMAN

IF WE COULD BE
TWICE YOUNG AND TWICE OLD.
WE COULD
CORRECT OUR MISTAKES.

There comes a time in every Salome's life when she should no longer be DROPPING THE LAST VEIL.

HARVEY FIERSTEIN

The older I grow, the more I listen to people who don't TALK MUCH.

GERMAIN G. GLIDDEN

Never too late to learn some EMBARRASSINGLY basic, stupidly obvious things about oneself.

ALAIN DE BOTTON

Wine doesn't make us any younger. Neither does carrot juice.

WINE IT IS THEN.

It is time I STEPPED ASIDE for a less experienced and less able man.

SCOTT ELLEDGE

By the time you read this, you'll be older than you remember.

CHUCK PALAHNIUK

When mathematicians turn 60, they disintegrate.

When sewage workers turn 60, they waste away.

When I die, I want to go peacefully like my grandfather did – in his sleep.

NOT YELLING AND SCREAMING LIKE THE PASSENGERS IN HIS CAR.

JACK HANDEY

Tomorrow I shall be sixty-nine, but I do not seem to care. I did not start the affair, and I have not been consulted about it at any step.

WILLIAM DEAN HOWELLS

Old is always fifteen years from now.

BILL COSBY

Do they sell Alphabetti Spaghetti in large type?

You know you are 60 when caravans don't seem such an odd idea after all.

I recently had my ANNUAL PHYSICAL EXAMINATION, which I get once every seven years, and when the nurse weighed me, I was SHOCKED to discover how much stronger the Earth's gravitational pull has become since 1990.

DAVE BARRY

Don't think of it as getting hot flushes. Think of it as your inner child playing with matches.

When violinists turn 60, they become UNSTRUNG.

Twenty can't be expected to tolerate sixty in all things, and sixty gets bored stiff with twenty's eternal love affairs.

EMILY CARR

LIFE is one long process of getting tired.

When policemen turn 60, they cop out.

You know you are 60 when you buy 3 pairs of the same trousers at once just in case they stop making them.

They say "Life is like riding a bicycle. You don't fall off unless you stop pedalling." I think I need stabilisers.

PEOPLE MATURE WITH AGE AND EXPERIENCE.
I hope I more resemble a
FINE WINE THAN BAD VINEGAR.

RICK KAPLAN

GIVE UP WITH HEALTHY FOODS – YOU NEED THE PRESERVATIVES.

TOP TIP

Don't stop half way up the stairs.
YOU'LL NEVER REMEMBER WHICH WAY
YOU WERE GOING.

An old man sees a friend sitting on a park bench WEEPING.

"How have things been with you Bob?" he asks his older friend.

"Great. I just married a BEAUTIFUL YOUNG WOMAN."

"Wonderful! But then why are you crying?"

"I CAN'T REMEMBER WHERE I LIVE."

Gray hair is God's graffiti.

BILL COSBY

When swimmers turn 60. they have a stroke.

Gran threw away her
BOURBONS, CUSTARD CREAMS
and ICED RINGS. Then she
continued her phone conversation
with tech support, saying,
"THERE, I'VE PUT ALL MY COOKIES
IN THE BIN. WHAT NEXT?"

I DON'T HAVE A BEER BELLY.
*I have a burgundy belly and it cost me
a lot of money.*
CHARLES CLARKE

A 60-year-old bald man went to the barbers. After his trim, he was shocked at the £20 bill. The barber said,

"IT WAS £5 FOR THE TRIM AND A £15 SEARCH FEE."

The years a woman subtracts from her age are not lost. They are added to the ages of other women.

DIANE DE POITIERS

I'm a walking library of facts... I've just lost my LIBRARY CARD.

You know you are 60 when you think "Deal or no Deal" requires skill.

An elderly couple were eating lunch at a restaurant. First the man ate his appetizer, then his main, and then finally his dessert. All the while with his wife just looking on, not even touching her food.

A concerned waitress approached the woman and asked if there was anything she could get for her. "No thank you," came her answer, "it's his turn for the teeth."

Age before beauty,
said the devil as he threw his
grandmother off the stairs.

GERMAN PROVERB

Like a lot of fellows around here, I have a furniture problem. My chest has fallen into my drawers.

BILLY CASPER

HE HAD DECIDED TO LIVE FOREVER, OR DIE IN THE ATTEMPT.

JOSEPH HELLER

Some day you will be old enough to start reading fairy tales again.

C.S. LEWIS

My memory's not as good as it used to be. Also, my memory's not as good as it used to be.

I'm at the age where food has taken the place of sex in my life. In fact, I'VE JUST HAD A MIRROR PUT OVER MY KITCHEN TABLE.

RODNEY DANGERFIELD

I DON'T MIND BEING IT

(age 60) I just don't like

SAYING IT.

DOLLY PARTON

Don't go all out or you'll end up all in.

You know you are 60 when
you no longer think of speed limits
AS A CHALLENGE.

It sounds quite flattering to be called a
SEXAGENARIAN.

What's the difference between a
clown and a man having a
MID-LIFE CRISIS?
The clown knows he's wearing
ridiculous clothes.

I've got a sizeable retirement nest egg. ITS AN OSTRICH EGG, and it's going to make an omelette so big that it'll produce enough leftovers for decades.

JAROD KINTZ

I DONT HAVE TIME to think about age. There are so many other things to do.

URSULA ANDRESS

YOU KNOW YOU ARE 60 when all you can SINK YOUR TEETH INTO is a glass.

I'VE LEARNT HOW TO PREVENT WRINKLES.

JUST EAT UNTIL THEY FILL OUT.

Retirement is having
nothing to do
and someone always
keeping you from it.

ROBERT BRAULT

AGE IS ALL IN
THE MIND.
The trick is to
stop it leaking
into your body.

You know you are 60 when you watch the 10 o'clock news by choice. Or you miss it because you were in bed at 9.

When theatre directors turn 60, they make a BIG PRODUCTION OF IT.

Grant me the senility to forget the people I never liked anyway, the good fortune to run into the ones I do, and THE EYESIGHT TO TELL THE DIFFERENCE.

The older I grow,
the more I distrust
the familiar doctrine that
age brings wisdom.

H.L. MENCKEN

The great thing
about getting
older is that you
don't lose all
the other ages
you've been.

MADELEINE L'ENGLE

You know
you are
60 when
you try to
enter your
password
on the
microwave.

You know you are 60 when buying a lawnmower is a TREAT RATHER THAN A NECESSITY.

Wisdom doesn't necessarily come with age. Sometimes age just shows up all by itself.

TOM WILSON

I HAVE ALWAYS PAID INCOME TAX. I object only when it reaches a stage when I am threatened with having nothing left for my old age – which is due to start NEXT TUESDAY OR WEDNESDAY.

NOEL COWARD

In youth we run into difficulties. In old age difficulties run into us.

BEVERLY SILLS

A man of sixty has spent twenty years in bed and over three years in eating.

ARNOLD BENNETT

A retired husband is often a wife's full-time job.

ELLA HARRIS

Who would be young in age, must in youth be sage.

GERMAN PROVERB

Middle age is the AWKWARD PERIOD when Father Time starts catching up with Mother Nature.

HAROLD COFFIN

WHEN GOLFERS TURN 60,

THEY LOSE THEIR DRIVE.

There was no respect for youth when I was young, and now that I am old, there is no respect for age - I missed it coming and going.

J.B. PRIESTLY

A key ring is a handy little gadget that allows you to lose all your keys at once.

NO ONE has yet been able to figure out at just what age a bachelor becomes confirmed.

At sixty, I know little more about wisdom than I did at thirty, but I know a great deal more about folly.

MASON COOLEY

There must be a day or two in a mans life when he is the precise age for something important.

FRANKLIN P. ADAMS

In youth we are plagued by desire; in later years, by the desire to feel desire.

MIGNON MCLAUGHLIN

You know you are 60 when you care less about when the pub closes than the chemists.

It's OK, you're only 11 ³/₄ in dog years.

When programmers turn 60, they decompile.

You have to stay in shape.

My grandmother, she started walking five miles a day when she was 60. She's 97 today and we don't know where the heck she is.

ELLEN DEGENERES

The only thing that goes **0-60** these **days** is the scales.

When electricians turn 60, they do it until it Hz.

Been there, done that, forgot all about it.

I'm not sixty, I'M "SEXTY".

DOLLY PARTON

I feel like my body has gotten totally out of shape, so I got my doctor's permission to join a FITNESS CLUB and start exercising. I decided to take an aerobics class for seniors. I bent, twisted, gyrated, jumped up and down, and perspired for an hour. But, by the time I got my leotard on, the class was over.

You know you are 60 when you can easily choose which bridges to mend and which to burn.

ITS ABSENT-MINDEDNESS when you forget, but it's gross negligence when your wife forgets.

If I see something SAGGING, BAGGING AND DRAGGING, I'm going to NIP IT, TUCK IT AND SUCK IT.

DOLLY PARTON

When you are 60 your
HAIR STARTS GETTING HEAVY.
It falls into your head and
starts coming out your
ears and nose.

JUST 'CAUSE THERE'S SNOW ON THE ROOF DOESN'T MEAN THERE'S NOT A FIRE INSIDE.

BONNIE HUNT

Bi-focals, tri-focals, what comes next?

The only time you really live fully is from THIRTY TO SIXTY. The young are slaves to dreams; the old servants of regrets. Only the middle-aged have all their five senses in the

KEEPING OF THEIR WITS.

THEODORE ROOSEVELT

Forget the block – when you're sixty, you've been around the entire neighbourhood a few times.

DANE PEDDIGREW

You know you are 60 when you START LYING ABOUT YOUR CHILDREN'S AGES.

Right now I'm having amnesia and déjà vu at the same time. I think I've forgotten this before.

STEVEN WRIGHT

When you get to my age, life seems little more than one long march to and from the lavatory.

JOHN MORTIMER

At the age of six I wanted to be a cook. At seven I wanted to be Napoleon. And my ambition has been growing steadily ever since.

SALVADOR DALI

You know you are 60 when every morning feels like the MORNING AFTER.

Age gives good advice when it is no longer able to give a bad example.

ALBANIAN PROVERB

AGE IS A BAD TRAVELLING COMPANION.

TRADITIONAL PROVERB

A middle-aged chap is advised to take up sport by his doctor, so he decides to play tennis. After a couple of weeks his wife asks him how he's doing.

He replies, "When I'm on the court and I see the ball speeding towards me, my brain immediately says, 'To the corner! Back hand! To the net! Smash! Go back!'"

"Great!" says his wife.

"But then my body says, 'Who? Me? Stop talking rubbish.'"

Don't you stay at home of evenings? Don't you love a cushioned seat in a corner, by the fireside, with your **SLIPPERS ON YOUR FEET?**

OLIVER WENDELL HOLMES

RETIREMENT: *It's nice to get out of the rat race, but you have to learn to get along* **WITH LESS CHEESE.**

GENE PERRET

Don't fool yourself that important things can be put off till tomorrow; they can be put off forever, or not at all.

MIGNON McLAUGHLIN

89

YOU KNOW YOU ARE 60
when you purchase
moisturiser by
THE CASE
instead
of by
THE JAR.

I'm old enough and cranky enough now that if someone tried to tell me what to do, **I'D TELL THEM WHERE TO PUT IT.**

DOLLY PARTON

You can take no credit for beauty at sixteen. But if you are beautiful at sixty, it will be your soul's own doing.

MARIE STOPES

No, that is the great fallacy: the wisdom of old men. They do not grow wise. They grow careful.

ERNEST HEMINGWAY

You know you are 60 when you NO LONGER NEED A SPOON TO STIR YOUR TEA. You just pour the milk in and let your shaky hand do the job.

Of all weights, old age is the HEAVIEST.

WELSH PROVERB

He who runs in his youth, trots in his old age.

SPANISH PROVERB

YOU'RE 60?

NO, YOU ARE JUST A 20-YEAR-OLD WITH 40 YEARS OF EXPERIENCE.

Here I sit, alone and sixty,

Bald, and fat, and full of sin,

Cold the seat and loud the cistern,

As I read the Harpic tin.

ALAN BENNETT

Wrinkled **WAS NOT** one of the things I wanted to be when I grew up.

When chauffeurs turn 60, they **LOSE THEIR DRIVE.**

HE HAS A PROFOUND RESPECT FOR OLD AGE. ESPECIALLY WHEN IT'S BOTTLED.

GENE FOWLER

EVERYTHING SLOWS DOWN WITH AGE,

except the time it takes cake and ice cream to reach your hips.

JOHN WAGNER

Don't confuse having a clear conscience with having a bad memory.

You can't be a model at age 60, but you certainly CAN BE AN ACTRESS.

EVA HERZIGOVA

I call it my SNAPDRAGON years. If it hasn't SNAPPED, it's DRAGGIN'.

A man's age commands RESPECT; a woman's demands TACT.

IT'S SAD WHEN THE KIDS LEAVE HOME. It's even sadder when you're enjoying your 60s and they divorce and MOVE BACK.

Preparation for old age should begin not later than one's teens.

A LIFE WHICH IS EMPTY OF PURPOSE

until 65 will not suddenly become filled on retirement.

DWIGHT L. MOODY

When cutting, look at the age of the machete.

NIGERIAN PROVERB

You're only as young as the last time you changed your mind.

TIMOTHY LEARY

"Well done Dad, I'm so proud of you. I noticed that when you sneeze, you've finally learned to put your hand in front of your mouth."

"Of course I have, otherwise I'd lose my false teeth."

I THINK, THEREFORE I STILL AM.

ELLIOT PRIEST

You know you are 60 when you haven't worn jeans for 10 years.

THE FIRST THIRTY years of life give us the text; the next thirty supply the commentary on it.

If old age was the same as wisdom, any old donkey would be a celebrated Justice.

PORTUGUESE PROVERB

A woman walked up to a little old man rocking in a chair on his porch. "I couldn't help noticing how happy you look." she said. "What's your secret for a long happy life?"

"I SMOKE 60 CIGARETTES A DAY." he said. "I ALSO DRINK A CASE OF WHISKY A WEEK. EAT FATTY FOODS AND NEVER EXERCISE."

"THAT'S AMAZING." the woman said. "How old are you?"

"Twenty-six."

AT 60,
"CHASING GIRLS"
refers almost exclusively
to GRANDDAUGHTERS.

GREG TAMBLYN

They talk about the economy this year. Hey, my hairline is in RECESSION, my waistline is in INFLATION. Altogether, I'm in a DEPRESSION.

RICK MAJERUS

He who eats a PARTRIDGE in his youth will only be left with FEATHERS in his old age.

SPANISH PROVERB

The four stages of man are infancy, childhood, adolescence, and OBSOLESCENCE.

ART LINKLETTER

When you are young, you want to be the master of your fate and the captain of your soul. When you are older, you will settle for being the master of your weight and the captain of the bowls team.

I'm between the age when time marches on and time runs out.

Retirement means goodbye tension. hello pension!

Age improves wine, compound interest and nothing else I can think of.

T. HARRY THOMPSON

From September to August drink the old wine and leave the must to age.

SICILIAN PROVERB

WHEN TRANSLATORS TURN 60, THEY BECOME LOST FOR WORDS.

Middle age is when work is a lot less fun and fun is a lot more work.

Men come of age at sixty, women at fifteen.

JAMES STEPHENS

I think my body is expanding to hold all the wisdom I've acquired.

When fortune tellers turn 60, they lose their vision.

The best time to start thinking about your retirement is JUST BEFORE YOUR BOSS DOES.

Sex appeal is 50% what you've got and 50% what people think you've got.

SOPHIA LOREN

Now, five years is nothing in a man's life except when he is very young and very old...

PEARL S. BUCK

You know you are 60 when you stoop to tie your shoes and wonder what else you can do WHILE YOU'RE DOWN THERE.

WHEN IS A 60-YEAR-OLD'S BEDTIME?

THREE HOURS

AFTER THEY FALL ASLEEP IN FRONT OF THE TV.

Every once in a while, you LIVE LONG ENOUGH to get the respect that people didn't want to give while you were trying to become a SENIOR CITIZEN.

GIL SCOTT-HERON

Marrying an old bachelor is like buying second-hand furniture.

H. JACKSON BROWN, JR

It's not age as much as the experiences I have had.

TONY CURTIS

You know you are 60
when your phone remembers
MORE THAN YOU DO.

You know you are
60 WHEN YOU KNOW
WHY IT'S CALLED
"DIALLING A NUMBER".

YOU DO LIVE OLDER WITH BRAN, BUT YOU SPEND THE LAST 15 YEARS ON THE TOILET.

ALAN KING

My arms are now too short to read the newspaper.

When bankers turn 60, they want to be a loan.

Artificial intelligence is a wonderful thing. I told my computer that today I was 60, and it said I NEEDED AN UPGRADE.

There's never enough time to do all the nothing you want.
BILL WATTERSON

The dangerous age is when men begin to regret the sins they didn't commit.

IS THE MIDNIGHT OIL RUNNING OUT AT 9PM?

Of course I'm against sin; I'm against anything that I'm TOO OLD TO ENJOY.

Life is like a bar of soap – once you think you've got a hold of it, it slips away.

A MAN SAID TO HIS FRIEND, "I'VE JUST BOUGHT A NEW HEARING AID. IT COST ME FOUR THOUSAND POUNDS, BUT IT'S THE BEST THERE IS." "WHAT KIND IS IT?" ASKED HIS FRIEND. "TWELVE THIRTY."

I see a lot of new faces, ESPECIALLY ON THE OLD FACES.

JOHNNY CARSON

NOW YOU'LL STOP LOOKING FORWARD TO FATHER CHRISTMAS AND START LOOKING LIKE HIM.

Man is like
palm-wine:
when young,
SWEET BUT
WITHOUT STRENGTH;
in old age,
STRONG BUT HARSH.

CONGOLESE PROVERB

Sometimes it's
hard to tell if
retirement is
A REWARD for a
lifetime of hard
work or
A PUNISHMENT.

TERRI GUILLEMETS

After a lifetime of wine,
women and song,
the good news is
YOU DON'T HAVE TO
GIVE UP SINGING.

There is a direct relationship between age and the amount of noise you make when getting up.

JANET PERIAT

I don't worry about losing my looks. It's finding them on someone else that worries me.

SIMON MUNNERY

I hope to die right in the middle of a song and right on the stage doing what I love to do. I HOPE TO BE ABOUT 120 WHEN THAT HAPPENS.

DOLLY PARTON

People are so busy lengthening their lives with exercise they don't have time to live them.

JONATHAN MILLER

In a man's middle years there is SCARCELY A PART OF THE BODY he would hesitate to turn over to the proper authorities.

E.B. WHITE

When men reach their sixties and retire, they go to pieces. Women go

RIGHT ON COOKING.

GAIL SHEEHY

I look forward to growing old and wise and audacious.

GLENDA JACKSON

Old age is desired, but when it comes, it's detested.

SICILIAN PROVERB

You know you are 60 when you do just as much as ever, BUT WOULD RATHER NOT.

You know you are 60 when senior moments start running into hours.

KNOWLEDGE is knowing a tomato is a fruit; WISDOM is not putting it in a fruit salad.

MILES KINGTON

Now that I'm over sixty I'm veering toward RESPECTABILITY.

SHELLEY WINTERS

The older you get the stronger the wind gets - and it's always in your face.

JACK NICKLAUS

You can be optimistic at your age. The glass really is half full. It needs to be to SOAK YOUR DENTURES.

You know you are 60 when you think a hard drive means avoiding road works on the high street.

You know you are 60 when you think that "Googling it" is something to do with cricket.

Experience is what you get when you DIDN'T GET WHAT YOU WANTED.

RANDY PAUSCH

AGE DOES NOT GIVE SENSE, IT ONLY MAKES ONE GO SLOWLY.

FINNISH PROVERB

Whether you are sixteen or over sixty, remember, understatement is the rule of a fine makeup artist.

HELENA RUBINSTEIN

When you were in school, was History called Current Affairs?

Old age is cruel for whores and magicians.

SPANISH PROVERB

FINALLY, YOUR SUPPLY OF BRAIN CELLS IS DOWN TO a manageable size.

Intelligence is in the head, not in the age.

AZERBAIJANI PROVERB

For his wife's 60th birthday party, a man ordered a cake with the inscription:

"You are not getting older, you are just getting better."

Asked how he wanted the message arranged, he said,

"Just put 'You are not getting older' at the top and 'You are just getting better' at the bottom."

It wasn't until the man was ready to serve the cake that he discovered that it read:

"YOU ARE NOT GETTING OLDER AT THE TOP. YOU ARE JUST GETTING BETTER AT THE BOTTOM."

You know you are 60 when you can live without sex but NOT WITHOUT GLASSES.

I've got enough crow's feet to start a bird sanctuary.

KATHY LETTE

Please note that once you hit 60, wearing hats is optional and not a legal requirement.

You know you are 60 when you
READ THIS BOOK
hoping that none of it
APPLIES
TO YOU.